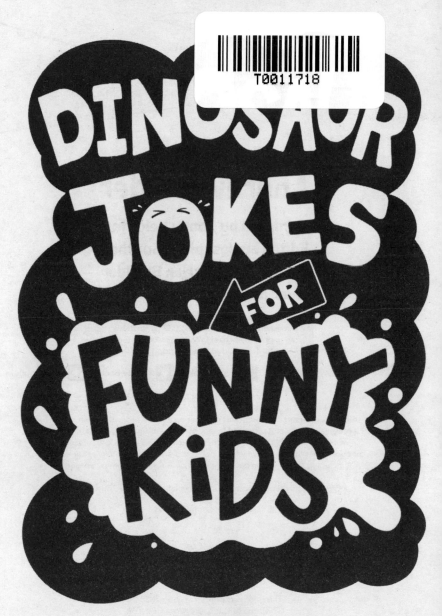

DINOSAUR JOKES FOR FUNNY KIDS

BUSTER BOOKS

Illustrated by
Andrew Pinder

Compiled by Jonny Leighton
Edited by Josephine Southon
Designed by Derrian Bradder
Cover design by Jake Da'Costa

First published in Great Britain in 2022 by Buster Books,
an imprint of Michael O'Mara Books Limited,
9 Lion Yard, Tremadoc Road, London SW4 7NQ

 www.mombooks.com/buster   f Buster Books   🐦 @BusterBooks   📷 @buster_books

A CIP catalogue record for this book is available from the British Library.

ISBN: 978-1-78055-907-0

2 4 6 8 10 9 7 5 3

This product is made of material from well-managed, FSC®-certified
forests and other controlled sources. The manufacturing processes
conform to the environmental regulations of the country of origin.

This book was printed in June 2023 by
CPI Group (UK) Ltd, Croydon, CR0 4YY.

MIX
Paper | Supporting
responsible forestry
FSC® C171272
FSC
www.fsc.org

CONTENTS

Introduction

What was the scariest prehistoric creature?

The Terror-dactyl.

Welcome to this bone-anza of the best-ever dinosaur jokes for funny kids.

In this book you will find over 250 dinomite jokes which will have you roaring with laughter – from knock-knock-asaurs and prehistoric LOLs to poop puns and caveman crackers.

If these jokes don't tickle your funny bone then nothing will. Don't forget to enraptor friends and family with your top gags and practise your comic timing.

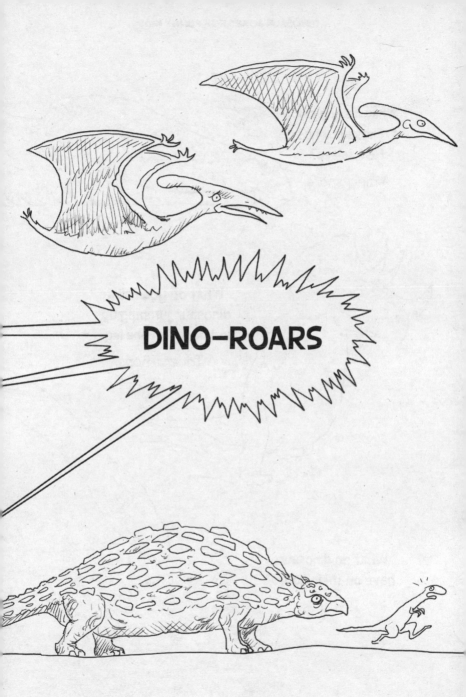

DINO-ROARS

What do you call a dinosaur who's fast asleep?

A dino-snore.

What do you call a dinosaur jumping up and down on one leg?

A Tricera-hops.

What do dinosaurs have on their floors?

Rep-tiles.

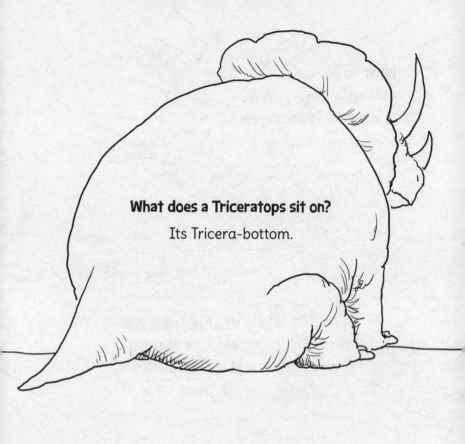

What does a Triceratops sit on?

Its Tricera-bottom.

**What does a T. rex use
to build a bookshelf?**

A dino-saw.

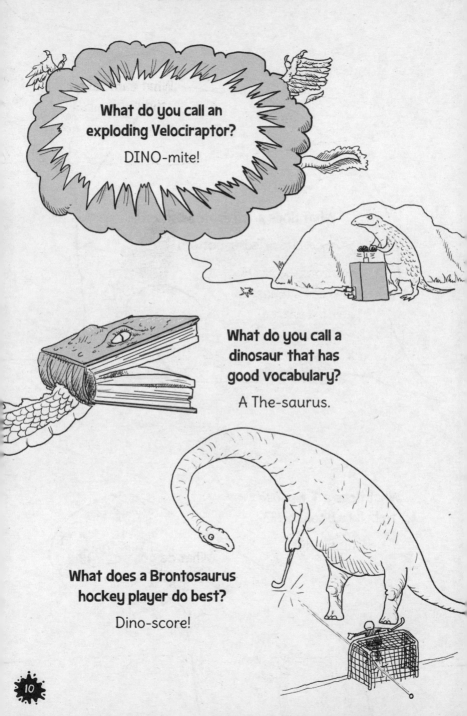

What do you call an exploding Velociraptor?

DINO-mite!

What do you call a dinosaur that has good vocabulary?

A The-saurus.

What does a Brontosaurus hockey player do best?

Dino-score!

**What came after
the dinosaurs?**

Their tails.

**What do you get if
you cross a dinosaur
with a wizard?**

A dino-sorcerer.

**What do you get if you
cross a Stegosaurus
with a pig?**

Jurassic pork.

**What do you call a dinosaur
with its eyes closed?**

A Do-you-think-he-saw-rus.

What do you call its dog?

A Do-you-think-he-saw-rus Rex.

What does a dinosaur play video games on?

A Rex-box.

Why can't a T. rex clap its hands?

Because it's extinct.

What do you call a dinosaur breaking wind?

A blast from the past.

**Why does a Brontosaurus
have a long neck?**

To avoid its
smelly feet!

What do you call a Spinosaurus with carrots in its ears?

Whatever you want –
it can't hear you.

What was the scariest prehistoric creature?

The Terror-dactyl.

What do you get when a dinosaur sneezes?

It snot worth thinking about.

What do you get in the middle of dinosaurs?

The letter 's'.

Why was the Allosaurus wearing a bandage?

It had a dino-sore head.

Why don't dinosaurs like to wash?

They're scared of meteor showers.

What makes more noise than a dinosaur?

Two dinosaurs.

What do you call a carnivore get-together?

A meat up.

Why can't you hear a Pterodactyl using the toilet?

Because the 'p' is silent.

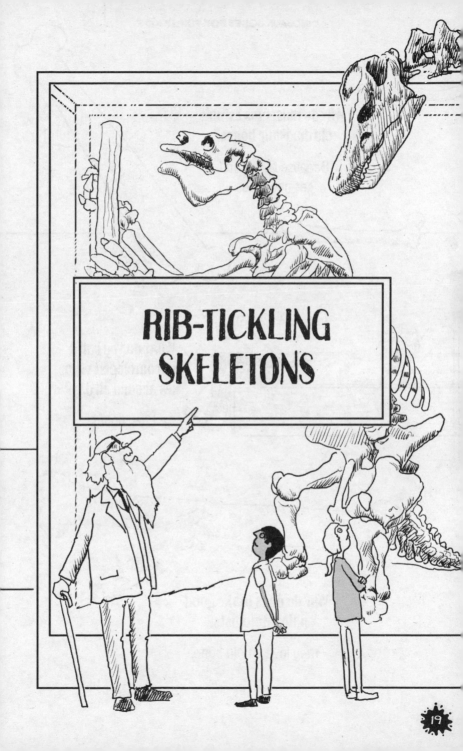

RIB-TICKLING SKELETONS

Why do museums exhibit
old dinosaur bones?

Because they can't
get new ones.

What do you call a
paleontologist who
lies around all day?

Lazy bones.

Why do dogs make good
paleontologists?

They love an old bone.

What kind of energy
do old bones need
to run on?

Fossil fuels.

What do you call it when a fossil
hunter organizes a party to
find a dinosaur's leg bone?

A shin dig.

Why do paleontologists keep
telling stories about dinosaurs?

They love a long tail.

What do you call a fossil
hunter with a spade?

Doug.

What do you call a fossil
hunter without a spade?

Douglas.

Did you hear about the haunted dinosaur museum?

It was full of Scare-a-dactyls.

What does the dinosaur museum guide say at the end of his tour?

"And the rest is history."

What did the dinosaur museum curator say when she looked up at a T. rex?

My-neck-is-saur.

23

What happened when a paleontologist finally found the last of the dinosaur bones?

He reached rock bottom.

Why didn't the dinosaur skeleton attack the museum visitors?

It was gutless.

Why should you never trust a dinosaur museum?

There are too many skeletons in its closet.

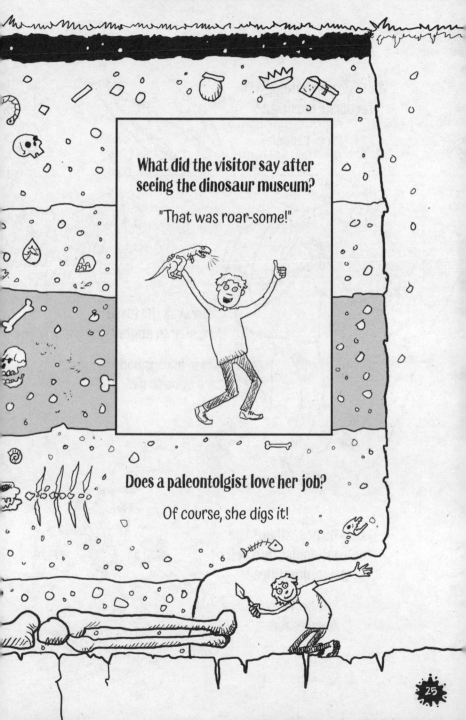

What did the visitor say after seeing the dinosaur museum?

"That was roar-some!"

Does a paleontolgist love her job?

Of course, she digs it!

What's a paleontologist's favourite musician?

A Veloci-rapper.

Why was the fossil hunter so angry?

He always had a bone to pick.

Did you hear about the paleontologist that fell down the stairs?

She broke her Ankylosaurus.

What happens when a paleontologist finds a dinosaur in the wild?

They run!

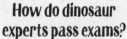

How do dinosaur experts pass exams?

With extinction.

Where do paleontologists get their tools?

From the Tricera-shops.

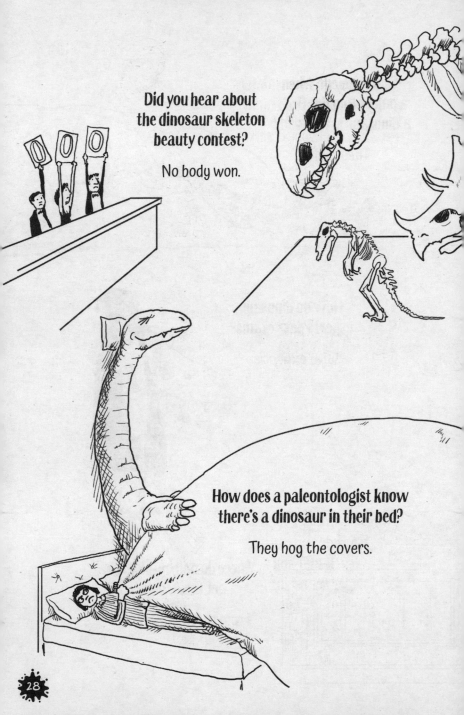

Did you hear about
the dinosaur skeleton
beauty contest?

No body won.

How does a paleontologist know
there's a dinosaur in their bed?

They hog the covers.

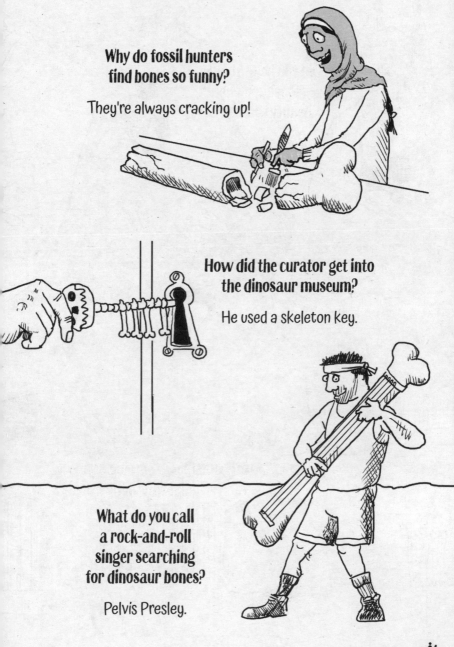

Why do fossil hunters find bones so funny?

They're always cracking up!

How did the curator get into the dinosaur museum?

He used a skeleton key.

What do you call a rock-and-roll singer searching for dinosaur bones?

Pelvis Presley.

Knock-knock-asaurs

Knock, knock!

Who's there?

Dinosaur.

Dinosaur, who?

Dinosaurs don't go "who", they go "ROAR!"

Knock, knock!

Who's there?

Terry.

Terry, who?

Terry-dactyl.

Knock, knock!

Who's there?

Dinosaurp.

Dinosaurp, who?

Ha ha, you said "dinosaur poo"!

Knock, knock!

Who's there?

Olive.

Olive, who?

Olive the dinosaurs are extinct.

Knock, knock!

Who's there?

Annie.

Annie, who?

Annie dinosaur will
swallow you whole!

Knock, knock!

Who's there?

Ida.

Ida, who?

Ida run quickly if
I were you, there's
a T. rex coming!

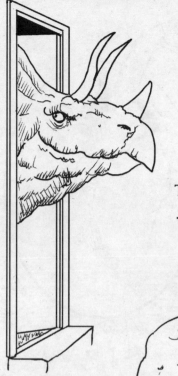

Knock, knock!

Who's there?

Try Sarah.

Try Sarah, who?

Try Sarah tops,
of course!

Knock, knock!

Who's there?

Interrupting dinosaur.

Interrupting dinosaur,
wh–?

ROARRRRRR!

Knock, knock!

Who's there?

Eggs.

Eggs, who?

**Eggs-stinct
dinosaurs.**

Knock, knock!

Who's there?

June.

June, who?

**June know any more
good dinosaur jokes?**

Knock, knock!

Who's there?

Icy.

Icy, who?

I see you, too!

Knock, knock!

Who's there?

Meteor.

Meteor, who?

Meet-your doom, dinosaurs!

Knock, knock!

Who's there?

Lena.

Lena, who?

Lena little closer and you'll get your arm bitten off!

Knock, knock!

Who's there?

Dinah.

Dinah, who?

Dinah-saur from her workout.

Knock, knock!

Who's there?

Kanye.

Kanye, who?

Kanye take a look at this fossil for me?

Knock, knock!

Who's there?

Will.

Will, who?

Will you let me in, there's a dinosaur chasing me!

Knock, knock!

Who's there?

Tyra.

Tyra, who?

Tyra-nnosaurus rex. Can I come in for a bite?

Knock, knock!

Who's there?

Dino.

Dino, who?

Dino you're scared to open the door, but I won't eat you, promise!

Knock, knock!

Who's there?

Dino.

Dino, who?

**Dino-mite is
what this joke is!**

Knock, knock!

Who's there?

Mike.

Mike, who?

**My Kentrosaurus escaped.
Help me find it!**

Clawsome Times

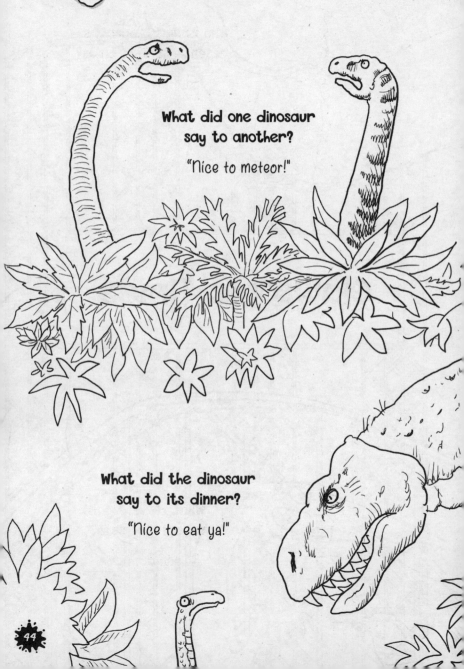

What did one dinosaur say to another?

"Nice to meteor!"

What did the dinosaur say to its dinner?

"Nice to eat ya!"

Who brings dinosaurs presents at Christmas?

Santa Claws.

What does the Easter Bunny bring dinosaurs?

Easter eggs-tinction.

What do you call a cool dinosaur?

Swagger-saurus.

Which dinosaur is the loudest sleeper?

The Tyranno-snorus.

What has three horns and sixteen wheels?

A Triceratops on roller-skates.

Why did the dinosaur cross the road?

To eat the chicken on the other side!

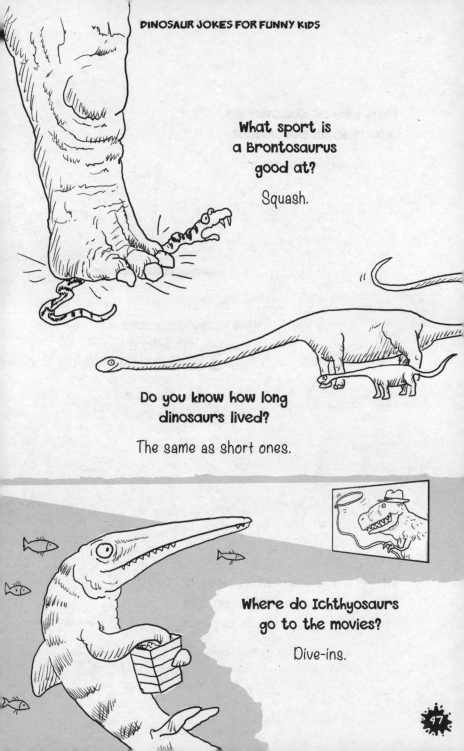

**What sport is
a Brontosaurus
good at?**

Squash.

**Do you know how long
dinosaurs lived?**

The same as short ones.

**Where do Ichthyosaurs
go to the movies?**

Dive-ins.

What kind of dinosaur do
you ride at the rodeo?

A buckin' Bronto.

How many dinosaurs
can you fit into a
cardboard box?

One – after that it's
not empty anymore.

What does a
dinosaur call
a porcupine?

A toothbrush.

What's the best way to raise a baby dinosaur?

With a crane.

49

Why do herbivores make great friends?

They leaf a good first impression.

Where can you find a Gallimimus sunbathing?

On the dino-shore.

What was the first dino-car invented?

The Model T. rex.

How do you upset a dinosaur?

Touch-a-sore-us spot.

How do dinosaurs like to dive into water?

Tri-belly-flops.

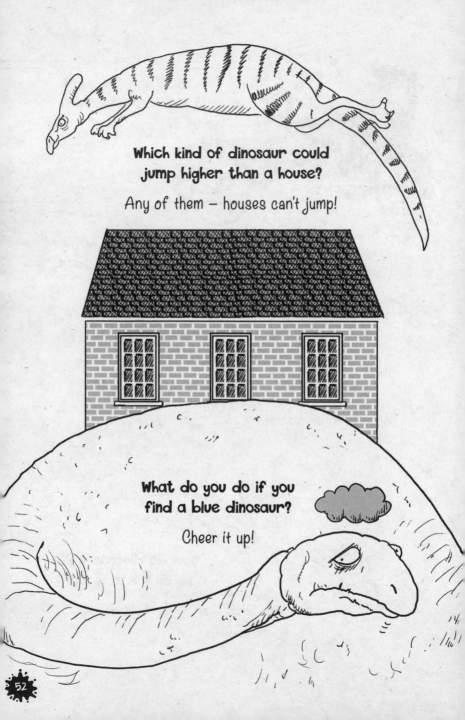

Which kind of dinosaur could jump higher than a house?

Any of them – houses can't jump!

What do you do if you find a blue dinosaur?

Cheer it up!

52

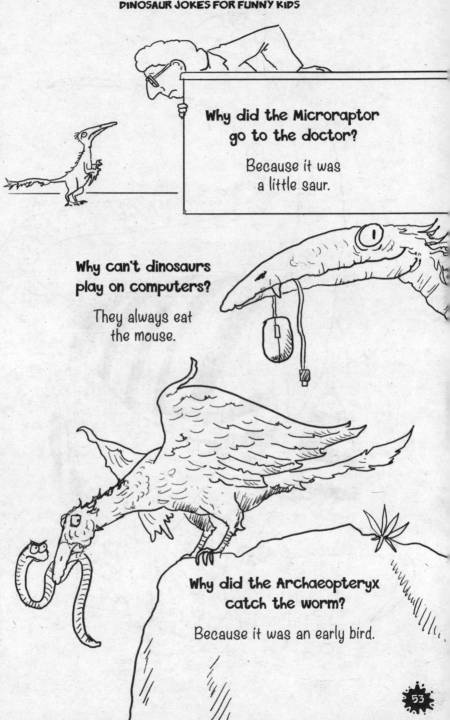

Why did the Microraptor go to the doctor?

Because it was a little saur.

Why can't dinosaurs play on computers?

They always eat the mouse.

Why did the Archaeopteryx catch the worm?

Because it was an early bird.

Jurassic Jokers

**Why did the dinosaur
find subtraction hard?**

It had to carry so many numbers.

**Where do dinosaurs
learn multiplication?**

Times Square.

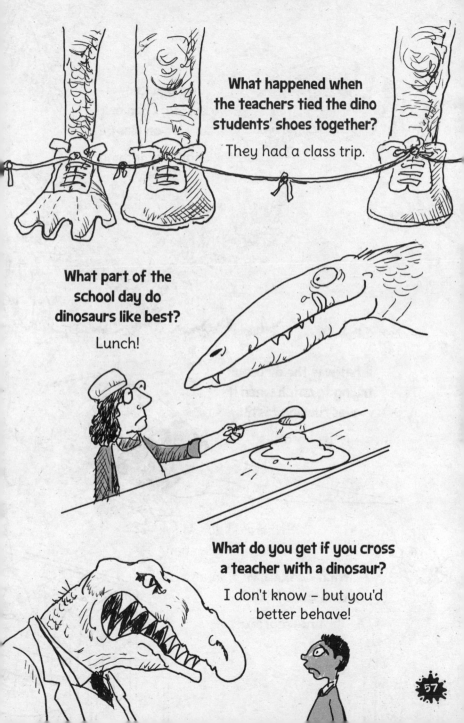

What happened when the teachers tied the dino students' shoes together?

They had a class trip.

What part of the school day do dinosaurs like best?

Lunch!

What do you get if you cross a teacher with a dinosaur?

I don't know – but you'd better behave!

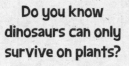

Do you know dinosaurs can only survive on plants?

That's something I've never herbivore!

What was the dinosaur trying to catch when it was running fast?

Its breath!

What do you call a dinosaur striker?

A Tyranno-score-us.

What do you call
a dinosaur who
lives in space?

An Astrosaurus.

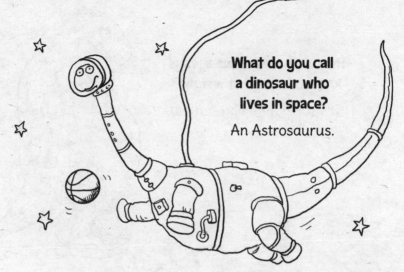

Why did the dinosaur
ballerina quit?

Because it was
tu-tu hard.

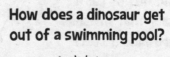

How does a dinosaur get
out of a swimming pool?

Wet.

How does a dinosaur always know how much it weighs?

It's surrounded by scales.

Why did the dinosaur's car come to a stop?

There was a flat Tyre-annosaurus.

What do you call a dinosaur that smashes everything it sees?

A Tyrannosaurus Wrecks.

What do you call a dinosaur that asks lots of deep questions?

A Philosiraptor.

Where did the dinosaur clown get a job?

At the carnivore.

Why did the Apatosaurus devour the factory?

It was a plant eater.

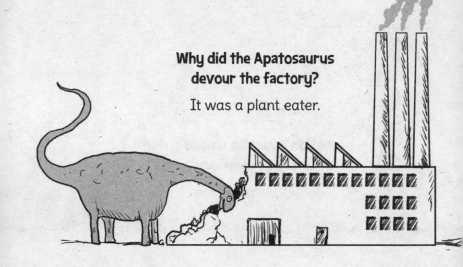

How do you invite a T. rex to a restaurant?

"Dinner, saur?"

How do dinosaurs like their steak?

ROAR!

What's worse than a giraffe with a sore throat?

A Diplodocus with a sore throat.

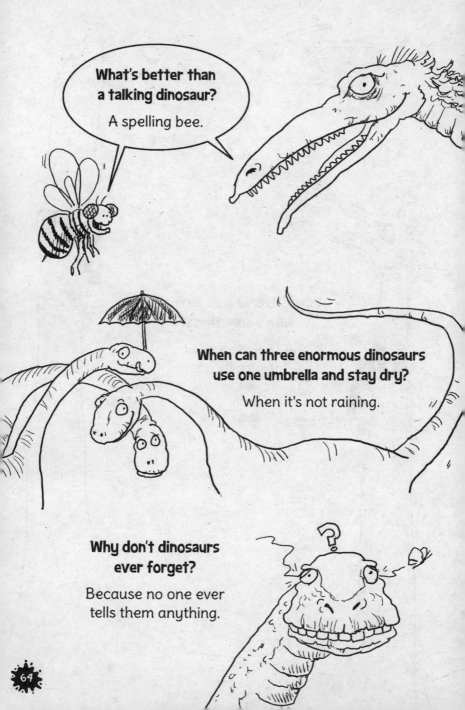

What's better than a talking dinosaur?

A spelling bee.

When can three enormous dinosaurs use one umbrella and stay dry?

When it's not raining.

Why don't dinosaurs ever forget?

Because no one ever tells them anything.

Why did the dinosaur bring a ladder to class?

It wanted to go to high school.

What's the difference between a dinosaur and a teacher?

One is scary, the other is a dinosaur.

Why did the dinosaur eat my homework?

Because it had also eaten the dog.

Prehistoric LOLs

What's the difference
between a dinosaur
and a caveman?

About 60 million years.

What time is it when
a mammoth sits
on your igloo?

Time to get a
new igloo!

Why are sabre-toothed
cats so snooty?

They think they're
purr-fect.

Who does a sabre-toothed cat go out with?

His grrrrlfriend.

Why do woolly mammoths have trunks?

Because they'd look silly carrying suitcases.

Where do cavemen hang out?

At the Rock Club.

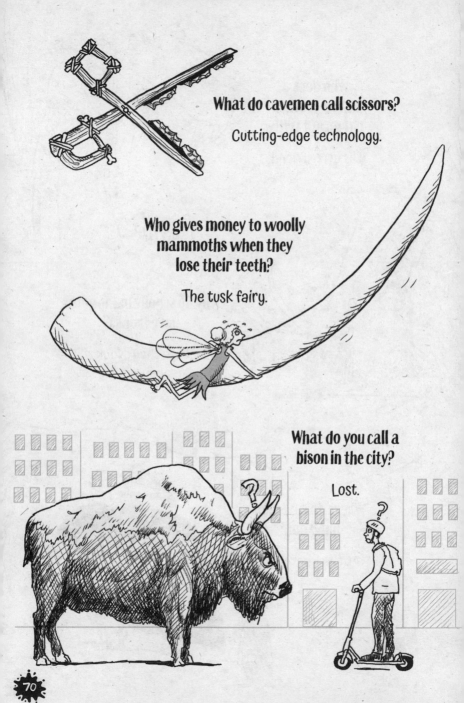

What do cavemen call scissors?

Cutting-edge technology.

Who gives money to woolly mammoths when they lose their teeth?

The tusk fairy.

What do you call a bison in the city?

Lost.

Why did the
woolly mammoth
cross the road?

They didn't have
chickens in the
Ice Age.

How do you stop a woolly
rhino from charging?

Unplug him.

What do you call
a caveman on
a surfboard?

A wave-man.

What do you do if a woolly
mammoth sneezes?

Dive into the snow and
hope for the best!

How do ground
sloths stay in shape?

Bear-obics.

Knock, knock!

Who's there?

Caveman.

Caveman, who?

**You can see who —
we haven't invented
doors yet!**

**Why was school
easier for
cavepeople?**

There was no
history to study.

What's stripy, bouncy and from Prehistoric times?

A sabre-toothed cat on a pogo stick.

What do you get when you cross a ground sloth and a sabre-toothed cat?

A slow leopard.

What did the sabre-toothed cat eat after having its tooth taken out?

The dentist!

What do you call
a bison that's
good at lying?

A bluff-alo.

Why don't sabre-toothed
cats like fast food?

They can't catch it.

What do you call a
woolly rhino in
a phone booth?

Stuck.

Why did the mammoth get thrown
out of the swimming baths?

It couldn't keep
its trunks up.

Why do woolly rhinos
have wavy fur?

They're hard to iron.

77

What do you call a sabre-toothed cat using a photocopier?

A copycat.

What do you call woolly mammoth poo?

Chocolate ice.

What do you call a caveman that takes the long route home?

A meander-thal.

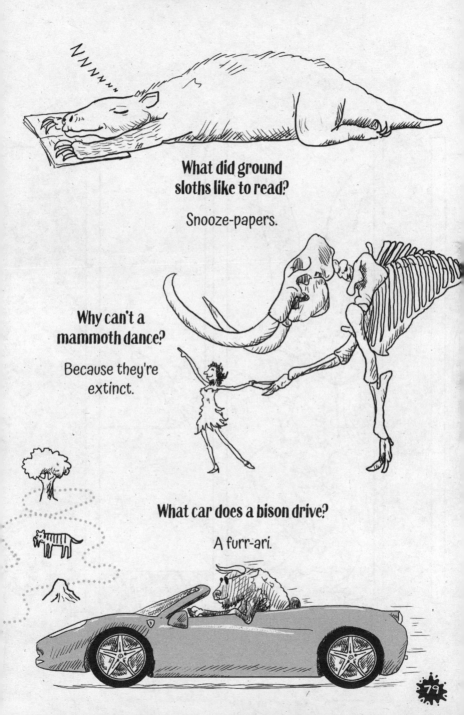

What did ground sloths like to read?

Snooze-papers.

Why can't a mammoth dance?

Because they're extinct.

What car does a bison drive?

A furr-ari.

Are you ready for a
dinosaur poo joke?

No, they ex-stink.

Are you ready for a
dinosaur poo joke, now?

No, they still ex-stink!

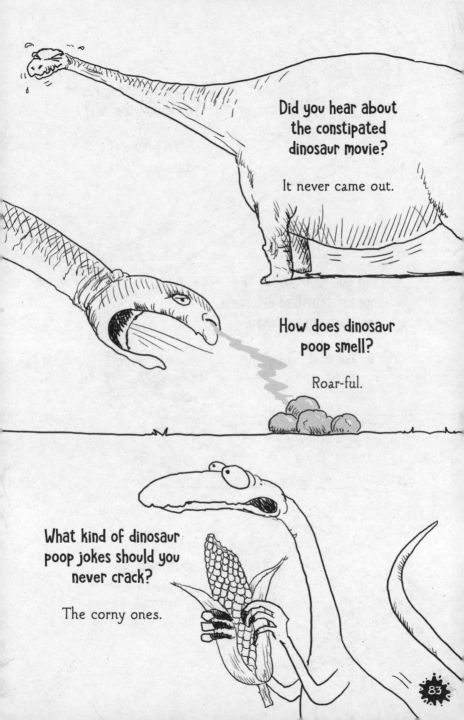

Did you hear about the constipated dinosaur movie?

It never came out.

How does dinosaur poop smell?

Roar-ful.

What kind of dinosaur poop jokes should you never crack?

The corny ones.

Why did the toilet paper
roll down the hill?

To get to the
dinosaur bottom.

Did you hear about the
dinosaur that had diarrhea
on the way to school?

It was running behind.

What time do
dinosaurs poo?

Poo-thirty.

Knock, knock!

Who's there?

Dinosaur did up.

Dinosaur did up, who?

Ew! Dinosaur did a poo!

Knock, knock!

Who's there?

Dinosaur poop.

Dinosaur poop, who?

Gross, you said
poo twice!

What's invisible and smells like dinosaurs?

A carnivorous dinosaur's fart.

How do dinosaurs prepare for a bubble bath?

They eat beans for dinner.

What do you call a farting dinosaur?

Stego-stinkus.

What does one fly say when the other one farts?

"Hey! I'm trying to eat here!"

What does one fly say to the other when it lands on dinosaur poop?

"Excuse me, is this stool taken?"

What do you call a pooing dinosaur?

Di-plop-docus.

What does a dinosaur do to warm up in bed?

It farts under the sheets.

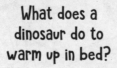

What do you call a
magic dinosaur dump?

Poodini.

What did the dinosaur poo
say to the dinosaur fart?

"You blow me away."

Why should you not tell too many dinosaur toilet jokes?

They'll make your cheeks hurt.

Why is dinosaur poop so rude?

It's always butting in.

Dinosaur poop jokes aren't everyone's favourites ...

... But they're a solid number two.

Knock, knock!

Who's there?

Dinosaurs eat mop.

Dinosaurs eat mop, who?

Dinosaurs eat your poo – gross!

Why did the dinosaur avoid the beach?

Because the sea weed.

Moresome Rawrsomes

Dinosaur 1: Why is your nose swollen?

Dinosaur 2: Because I was smelling a brose.

Dinosaur 1: Don't be silly, there's no 'b' in 'rose'.

Dinosaur 2: There was in this one!

Why do Mosasaurus live in saltwater?

Because pepper makes them sneeze.

How do you outrun a dinosaur?

You don't need to – you just have to run faster than your friend!

What do you call a wobbly dinosaur?

A Stagger-saurus.

What do dino-farmers grow?

Tricera-crops.

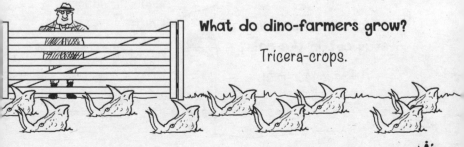

**Who do dinosaurs
hang out with?**

Their best pal-eontologist.

**What do you call a dinosaur
that loves embroidery?**

A dino-sewer.

**Which dinosaur can't
stay out in the rain?**

A Stegosaur-rust.

Where do dino fans like to eat?

At the diner-saur.

Who did the museum call when there was a break-in?

The Tricera-cops.

What type of snake does a baby dinosaur like to play with?

A rattlesnake.

A caveman had a great Ice Age joke to tell ...

... Shame it slipped his mind.

What do you say when you meet a two-headed dinosaur?

"Hello, hello!"

What did the doctor give to the dinosaur that couldn't stop breaking wind?

A kite.

Doctor, Doctor, there's an invisible dinosaur in the waiting room.

Tell him I can't see him.

What did the doctor give to the dinosaur with strawberries in its ear?

Cream.

How does a dinosaur
make an apple turnover?

Push it down a hill.

What's better
than a dinosaur?

A dinosaur with
chocolate!

Want to hear a joke
about a dinosaur
eating pizza?

Never mind, it's
too cheesy.

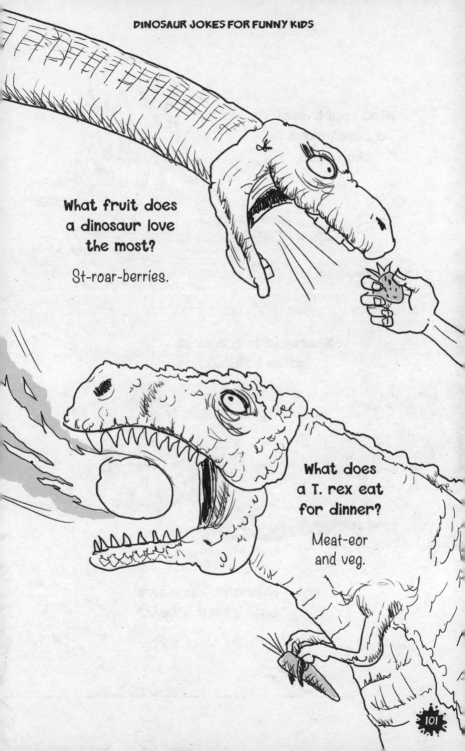

What fruit does a dinosaur love the most?

St-roar-berries.

What does a T. rex eat for dinner?

Meat-eor and veg.

What sport does
a Dimetrodon
like best?

Sailing.

Where do Spinosaurus
go on holiday?

Finland.

Where do dinosaurs
catch their flights?

At the scare-port.

Why do dinosaurs love the beach?

The sea always waves.

What does a Megalodon use to call its friends?

A shell-phone.

Silly Snicker-saurs

Why can't dinosaurs think about their past birthdays?

Because they're always thinking about the present.

What does every dinosaur birthday end with?

The letter 'y'.

What does a Triceratops get for its birthday?

One year older.

106

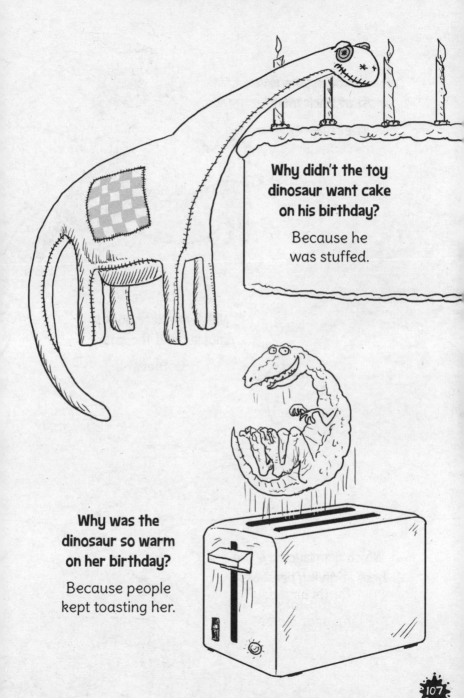

Why didn't the toy dinosaur want cake on his birthday?

Because he was stuffed.

Why was the dinosaur so warm on her birthday?

Because people kept toasting her.

What do dinosaurs love most at Christmas?

The tree-rex.

Which reindeer does a dinosaur like the least?

Comet.

Which dinosaurs are the best at giving presents?

Wrap-tors.

What kind of pictures do dinosaurs take on Christmas Day?

Elfies.

What does a Triceratops hang on its Christmas tree?

Horn-aments.

109

Who did the paleontologist go to the party with?

Any body he could dig up.

Why didn't the dinosaur skeleton go to the party?

It had no body to go with.

Where do dinosaur ghosts go on holiday?

The Boo-hamas.

Why did the dinosaur skeleton climb up a tree?

Because a dog was after his bones.

What do you call a dinosaur ghost?

A Try-to-scare-us.

What spell does a witch put on a dinosaur?

A T. hex.

Where does a dinosaur play the violin?

In a roar-chestra.

What part of a dinosaur is the most musical?

The scales.

What instrument does a fossil like the most?

The trombone.

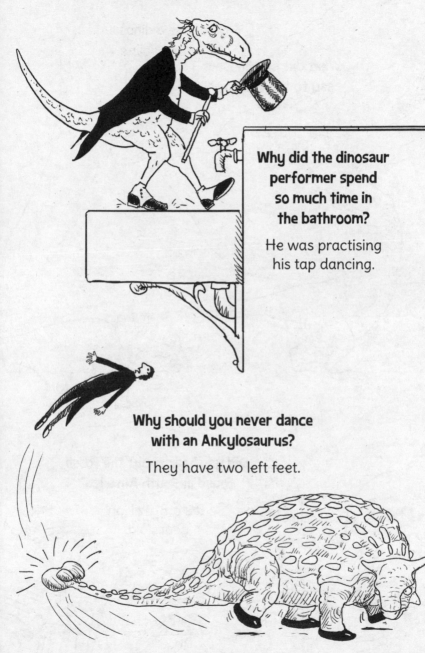

**Why did the dinosaur
performer spend
so much time in
the bathroom?**

He was practising
his tap dancing.

**Why should you never dance
with an Ankylosaurus?**

They have two left feet.

**What did the dinosaur
say to the volcano?**

Have a
lava-ly day!

**Did you hear about the fossil
found in South America?**

It's a Brazillion
years old.

Why can you never disguise a dinosaur?

They stick out like a saur thumb.

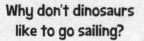

Why don't dinosaurs like to go sailing?

There are too many ship rex.

Final Funnies

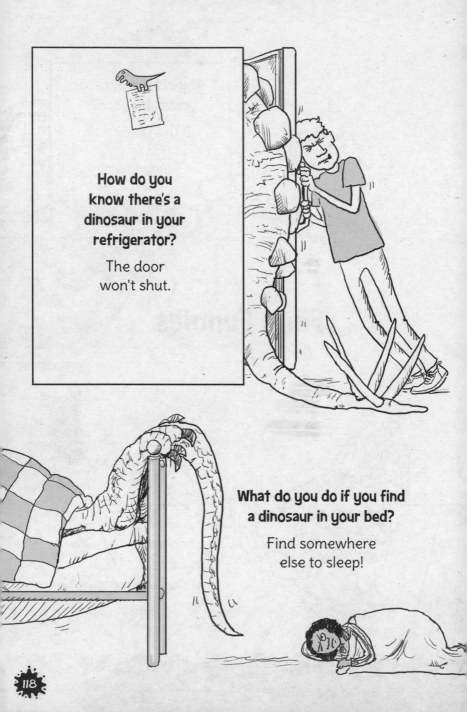

How do you know there's a dinosaur in your refrigerator?

The door won't shut.

What do you do if you find a dinosaur in your bed?

Find somewhere else to sleep!

Why did the dinosaur
cross the road?

It didn't – roads
hadn't been
invented yet!

Why did the dinosaur
take a bath?

Because it was
ex-stinky.

What do you get when a
dinosaur walks through
a strawberry patch?

Jam!

What do you call a group of singing dinosaurs?

A Tyranno-chorus.

What do you call a shy dinosaur?

A nervous-rex.

What do you call a dinosaur that never gives up?

A Tri-tri-triceratops.

Why did the T. rex go to the optician?

To buy some Tyrannosaurus specs.

What's as big as a dinosaur but weighs nothing?

Its shadow.

What do you call a fossil hunter who hates losing?

A saur loser.

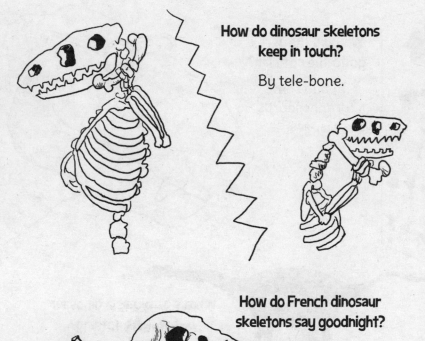

How do dinosaur skeletons keep in touch?

By tele-bone.

How do French dinosaur skeletons say goodnight?

"Bone nuit!"

What does a pirate say when he finds a dinosaur bone?

"Shovel me timbers!"

The other day, the paleontolgist was so excited, she thought she'd found a dinosaur leg ...

... But it was just a fossil arm.

What happens when two fossil hunters fall in love?

They go carbon dating.

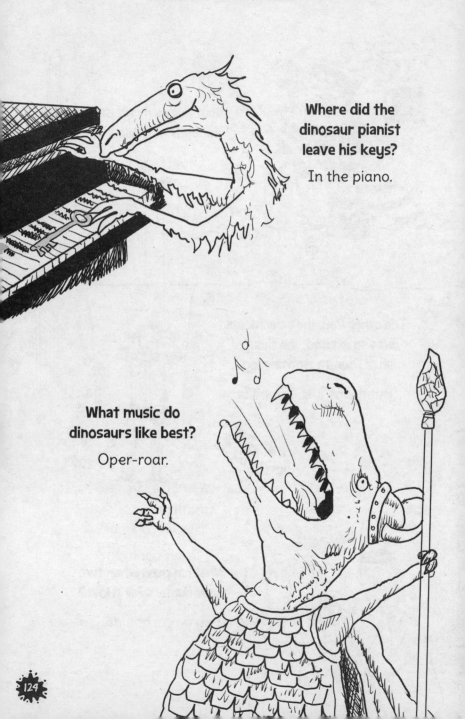

**Where did the
dinosaur pianist
leave his keys?**

In the piano.

**What music do
dinosaurs like best?**

Oper-roar.

Which instruments were missing from the dinosaur skeleton orchestra?

The organs.

What do a dinosaur's tooth and a piano have in common?

They can both B sharp.

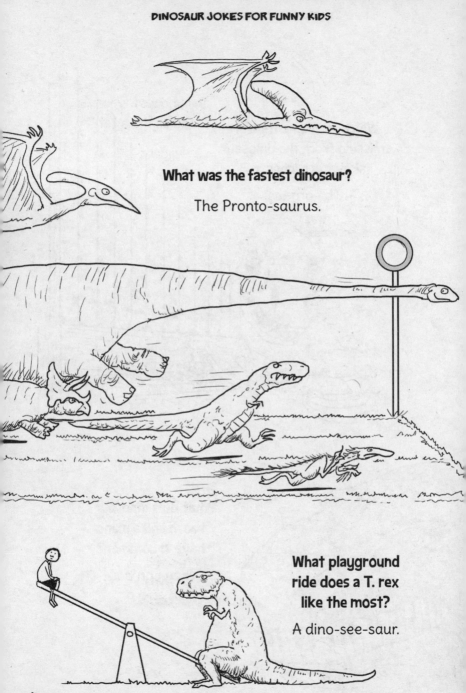

What was the fastest dinosaur?

The Pronto-saurus.

What playground ride does a T. rex like the most?

A dino-see-saur.

**What does a dinosaur
do on the toilet?**

Tricera-plops.

**What does an alien
dinosaur use to travel
through space?**

A flying dino-saucer.

**What do you call a
Velociraptor that
won't stop talking?**

A dino-bore.

127

ALSO AVAILABLE:

ISBN: 978-1-78055-908-7

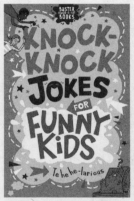

ISBN: 978-1-78055-785-4

ISBN: 978-1-78055-784-7

ISBN: 978-1-78055-708-3

ISBN: 978-1-78055-626-0

ISBN: 978-1-78055-624-6

ISBN: 978-1-78055-625-3